A Spelling Dictionary for Writers

Book 2

A Resource for Independent Writing

by Gregory Hurray

EDUCATORS PUBLISHING SERVICE

Cambridge and Toronto

Design by Regina Martine

Printed in the U.S.A.

ISBN 0-8388-2057-5

A Message to Students

"Look it up." This probably sounds familiar to you. Chances are, you'll need to look up a word that someone else has looked up before. The 5,000 words in this book make up about 95% of the words you use when you write. If you need to look something up, there is a 95% chance that you will find it here first.

Words are listed alphabetically. Some words have different forms, or inflections, that you may be likely to use as well. Some words may sound like another word with a different spelling. These are defined for you so that you do not confuse them. You may not find every word you look for. When that happens, try to find the word in a regular dictionary, and write it here. There is space for you to write your most favorite and frequently used words in between entries and the end of each section.

Keep this book in your desk, locker, or backpack. Take it with you to class and take it home for homework. Mark the words that you use most often. You will probably stop looking up certain words after a while. That means you've learned them—you have made them your own.

This book can help you even when you *don't know* which word you are looking for. The Thesaurus lists alternatives for words you may get tired of writing. There are many ways to say *big* or *small, happy* or *sad, like* or *dislike*. There are lists of words to describe things, people, and places. You may be looking for a particular holiday, color, sport, country, computer word, or career. You may be asked to write an abstract for your science project, a short answer to a social studies homework question, or an essay about the book you are reading in English class. This book can help you find the perfect word. If you find there are words you need often that are not in this book, write them in the spaces provided. You may also send suggestions for new entries to Educators Publishing Service, Inc. We may be able to add your words to the next printing of this book.

Write well and write often.

—Gregory Hurray

A Message to Teachers

This book is predicated on a very simple idea: students should be given access to words they need in their writing. According to studies by researchers such as E. Horn, Dewey, Fries, Rinsland, Fitzgerald, and others, a list of approximately 5,000 words accounts for nearly 95% of the words students in grades five through nine use in their compositions. Unfortunately, many of the words used most frequently by young writers have irregular or unpredictable spellings and cannot be sounded out. They must be recalled from memory, retrieved from a book or chart, or written down by a teacher.

Unlike most intermediate dictionaries, which often contain more than 50,000 entries and 1,000 or more pages, this volume is designed for maximum efficiency for the middle school student. It contains approximately 5,000 of the words most frequently used at the middle-school writing level, including a number of common inflected forms. These entries are based on published research and years of my own experience as a writing specialist and teacher in the public schools.

The thematic thesaurus adds a second dimension to the dictionary. These lists and word banks can facilitate descriptive, personal, as well as expository writing. These pages offer unique alternatives for overused words and expressions such as *big* and *small, a lot* and *a little, good* and *bad,* etc. Thematic lists help with writing about the major subjects, including literature, social studies, math, science, music, and art. Word banks for sports and activities, religions and holidays, computers and technology, family and relatives, and other themes, will help students write about current events in the world and in their own lives.

Throughout, the intent has been to give students an opportunity to take responsibility for their own learning, to nurture their emerging knowledge of English orthography, to encourage good spelling and research habits, and to make it easier for the classroom teacher to promote good writing practices. To the extent that we succeed in each of these endeavors, our time will be well spent.

—Gregory Hurray

Contents

Dictionary

A

a

a.m.

abandon

able
ability

abolish
abolitionist

about

above

abrupt
abruptly

absence
absent

absolute
absolutely

abundance
abundant

academic

academy

accept (*accept* a gift)
acceptable
accepted

access
accessible

accident
accidental

accommodate

accompany

accomplices

accomplish

according

account

accumulate

accurate
accurately

accuse
accused
accusation

accustomed

ache

achieve

acid

acknowledge

acquaintance
acquainted

acquire

acres

across

act
acting
actor

action
active
activity
activities

actual
actually

add
addition
additional

address

adequate
adequately

administration

admire

admission

admit

adolescence
adolescent

adopt
adoption

adult

advance
advanced

advantage

adventure
adventurous

advertise
advertising
advertisement

advice

advise

affairs

affect (to influence)

affection
affectionately

afford

afraid

Africa
African
African American

after

afternoon

afterward

again

against

age
aged

aggravate

aggressive
aggressively

ago

agony
agonizing

agree
agreed
agreement

agriculture

ahead

aid

aim

air (fresh *air*)

airplane

airport

aisle (down the *aisle*)

alarm

alcohol

alien

alike

alive

all

all right

alley

allow
allowed

almost

alone

along

alphabet

already

also

alternative

although

altogether

always

am

amaze
amazed
amazing

ambition
ambitious

amend

America
American

amidst

among

amount

amphibians

amuse
amusement
amusing

an

analysis
analyze

ancient

and

angry

animal

anniversary

announce
announcement

annoy
annoyed
annoying

annual

anonymous

another

answer

ant (small insect)

Antarctica

Australia

anticipate

antique

anxiety
anxious

any

anybody

anymore

anyone

anything

anyway

anywhere

apart

apartment

apiece

apologize

appalling

apparent
apparently

appear
appearance
appeared

applaud
applause

apple

apply
applying
applied
application

appointed
appointment

apologize
apology

appreciate
appreciation

approach

appropriate

approve
approved
approval

approximate
approximately

April

apron

Arabic

archaeology
archaeologist

architect
architecture

are
aren't

area

arena

argue
argument

arithmetic

arm

army

aroma

arose

around

arrange
arrangement

arrest
arrested

arrive

arrogant

arrow

art
artist

article

artificial

as

ashamed

ashes

Asia
Asian
Asian American

ask
asked

asleep

aspect

assemble
assembly

assign
assignment

assist
assistance
assistant

associate
associated
association

assortment

assume
assuming
assumption

assure

astonish
astonished

astounding

astronomy

at

ate (*ate* a meal)

athlete
athletic

Atlantic

atmosphere

attach
attached

attack

attempt

attend
attendance

attention

attic

attitude

attorney

attract
attracted
attractive
attraction

audience

auditorium

August
Aug.

aunt (*aunt* and uncle)

authentic

author

auto

autobiography

automatic
automatically

automobile

autumn

available

avenue

average

avoid

awake
awaken

award

away

awesome

awful

awhile

awkward

ax

B

baby
babies

back

background

backward

bacon

bacteria

bad
badly

bag

bait

bake

balance

ball

ballet

balloon

ballot

banana

band

bandanna

bandage

bang

bank

banner

bar

barber

bare

bark

barn

barrel

barrier

base
based

baseball

basement

basic
basically

basket

basketball

bass

bath

bathe

batter

battery

battle

battlefield

bay

be
being

beach

bean

bear
bearing

beard

beast

beat

beauty
beautiful

became
become

because

become

bed

bedroom

bedtime

bee
bees

beef

been

beets (the vegetable)

before

beg
begged

begin
began
beginning
begun

behave
behavior

behind

belief

believe
believable

bell

belong
belongings

beloved

below

belt

bench

bend
bent

beneath

benefit
beneficial

bent

berry (the fruit)

beside

best

bet

better

between

beyond

bicycle
bike

big
bigger
biggest

bill
billed
billing

bind

biography
biographical

biology
biological

bird

birth

birthday

bit

bite

bitter

bizarre

black

blackboard

blade

blame

blanket

blaze
blazing

bleed
bled

bless
blessing

blind

block
blocks

blood

bloom
blooming

blossoms

blow
blew

blue (the color)

boar (wild pig)

board (plank of wood)
boarding

boast

boat

body
bodies

boil

bold

bolt
bolted

bomb

bone
bones

book

booklet

boom
booming

boots

border

bore (to drill/to put
   someone to sleep)
bored

born

borrow

boss

both

bother
bothered

bottle

bottom

bough (tree limb)

bounce

bought
buy

bound

boundary
boundaries

bow

bowl

box
boxing

boy
boys

brace
braces

bracelet

brain

brake (on a bike)

branch

brave
bravery

bread

break (destroy)
broke
broken

breakfast

breath

breathe
breathing

breeze
breezy

brick

bridge

bridle

brief

bright
brighten

brilliant

bring
brought

broad

broke
broken

brook

broom

brother

brought
bring

brown

bruise

brush

bubble
bubbles

buck

bucket

buckle

bud
budding

Buddhism
Buddhist

buffalo

bug
bugs

build
building
built

bulb

bull

bulldog

bullet

bump

bunch

bundle

bureau

buried
bury

burglary

burn

burst

bury (place in the ground)
buried

bus

bush
bushes

bushels

business

busy

but

butter

butterfly

button

buy (in a store)
bought

by (written *by*)
bye (good-*bye*)

C

cabbage

cabin

cabinet

cable

cafeteria

cage

cake

calcium

calendar

calf

call
called

calm
calmly

calorie

calf
calves

camel

came
come

camera

camouflage

camp
camping

campaign

campfire

can
canned
canning

can
cannot
can't

canal

canary

cancer

candidate

candle

candy

cane

cannon

canoe
canoeing

cannot

can't

canyon

cap

capable
capability

capacity

capital (city, letter)

Capitol (building)

captain

captivate
captivating

capture

car

carbohydrate
carbohydrates

carbon

card

cardboard

care
caring

career
careers

careful
carefully

careless
carelessly

carnival

carpenter

carpet
carpeting

carriage

carrot

carry
carried
carries

cart

carve
carving

case

cassette

cast

castle

cat

catalog

catastrophe

catch
catching
caught

Catholic

cattle

caught
catch

cause
caused
causing

caution
cautious

cave

CD

cease

ceiling

celebrate
celebration

celery

cell
cellular

cement

cemetery

censor
censorship

cent (¢)
cents

center

centimeter

central

century
centuries

cereal

certain
certainly

certificate

chain

chair

chalk

challenge
challenging
challenger

champion
championship

chance

change

channel

chap
chapped

chapter

character
characteristics

charge

charm
charming

chart

chase

chat
chatting

cheap

check
checker

cheek

cheer
cheerful
cheerfully

cheese

chemical
chemistry

cherish

cherry
cherries

chest

chew
chews

chicken

chief
chiefs

child
children

chill
chilly

chimney
chimneys

Chinese

chip
chipped

chocolate

choice

choir

choke
choking

choose
choosing
chose

chop
chopped

chore

chorus

chose
choose

Christian
Christianity

Christmas

chuckle
chuckled

chum

church

cider

cigar

cigarette

circle
circling
circular

circuit

circular

circumstance
circumstances

circus

cities

citizen
citizenship

city
cities

civic

civil
civilian
civilization

claim

clamp

clanking

clap
clapping

class
classes

classic
classics

classmate

clay

clean

clear

clerk

cliff

climate

climb
climber

clock

close
closing

closet

closing

cloth

clothes
clothing

cloud

clown

club

clutch

coach

coal

coast

coat
coated

cocoa

coconut

code

coffee

coin

coincidence
coincidentally

cold

collapse
collapsing

collar

collect
collection

college

collide

colonel

colony
colonies

color
colorful

column

comb

combine
combination

come
coming
came

comedian
comedy

comfort
comfortable
comforting

comic
comical

command

commence
commencement

comment
commentary

commerce
commercial

commission

commit
committed

committee

common
commonly

commotion

communicate
communication

community

compact disc
CD

companion

company
companies

compare
comparison

compartment

compassion
compassionate

competition
competitive

complain
complaint

complete
completely

complex

complicated
complications

compliment (a nice
thing to say)

compose
composer
composition

compound

comprehend
comprehension

computer
computerized

conceal
concealed

conceited

concentrate
concentration

concept

concern
concerned

concert

concise

conclude
conclusion

condition
conditioner

conduct
conductor

cone

conference

confession

confidence
confident
confidential

conflict

confront

confuse
confusing
confusion

congratulate
congratulations

congress

conjunction

connect
connection

conquer

conscience

conscious
consciousness

consecutive

consent

consequence
consequences

consider
considerate
consideration

consists
consisted
consistent

constant
constantly

constitution

construct
construction

consume

contain
contained
container

contemplate
contemplation

content

contest

continent

continue

contract
contraction

contradiction
contradictory

contribute
contribution

control
controlled

controversy
controversial

conversation

crucial

convenience
convenient

convention
conventional

convey

convince
convincing

convinced

cook

cookie
cookies

cool

cooperate
cooperation

copies

copper

copy
copies

cord

corn

corner

corporate
corporation

correct
correction

correspond
correspondence

cost

costume

cottage

cotton

cough

could
couldn't

counselor
counseling

count

country

county

couple

coupon

courage
courageous

course

court

courteous
courtesy

cousin

cover
covered

cow
cows

cozy

crack
cracked

cradle
cradling

crash

crawl
crawled

crayon

crazy

creak (make a noise)

cream

create
creative
creativity

creature

creek (a brook)

creep
crept

crew

cried
cry

crime
criminal

critic
critical

croak

cross

crow

crowd
crowded

crown

crude

cruel
cruelty

cruise
cruising

crumb

crusade

crushed

cry
crying
cried

crystal

culture
cultural

cup

cure

curious
curiosity

currency

current
currently

curry

curtain

curve

custom
customs

customer

cut

cute

cycle

dad
daddy

daily

dam

damage

damp

dance

danger
dangerous

dare
daring

dark
darkness

dash

data

date

daughter

day
days

dazzle
dazzling

dead
deadly

deaf

deal

dear (*Dear* John)

death
deaths

debate
debating

debt

decade

deceased

deceive

December
Dec.

decent

decide
decision

deck

declare
declaration
declarative

decorate
decoration
decorator

decrease
decreasing

deed

deep

deer (the animal)

defeat
defeated

defect
defects

defend
defendant
defense
defensive

define
definition

definite
definitely

degree
degrees

delay

delectable

delegate
delegates

deliberate
deliberately

delicacy

delicate

delicious

delight
delighted
delightful

deliver
delivery

demand

democracy
Democrat

demolish

demonstrate

dense
density

dentist

deny
denied
denies

department

depend

deposits

depression
depressing

depth

descend

describe
describing
description

desert (the Sahara)

deserted

deserve

design
designed

desire

desk

desperate
desperately

despise

dessert (after dinner)

destination

destroy
destruction

detail

detect
detective

determine
determination

devastating
devastation

develop
developed
development

device

devil

devour
devoured

dew (moisture)

diagram

dialogue

diameter

diamond

diary

dictionary

die
died

diet

difference
different

difficult

dig

digest

digital

dignity

dilemma

dime

dinner

dinosaur

dip

direct
direction
director

dirt

disadvantage

disagree
disagreeable
disagreement

disappear
disappeared

disappointed
disappointing

disapprove

disaster
disastrous

disbelief

disc (compact *disc*)
disk (floppy *disk*)

discomfort

discourage
discouraged

discover

discriminate
discrimination

discuss
discussion

disease

disgrace

disguise

disgust
disgusted

dishes

dismay

dismiss

disobey

disorganized

display

dispute

dissolve

distance

distinct
distinctive

distinguish

distressed

distributed

disturb

disturbing

dive
dived
dove

divide

division

divorce

do
doing
don't

dock

doctor
Dr.

document

doe (female deer)

does
doesn't

dog

doing

doll

dollar

dome

dominate

done

don't

door

dot

double

doubt

dough (unbaked bread)

dove (a bird)

down

download

downstairs

dozen

Dr.

drag

dragon

drain

drama

drank

drink

draw
drawing

drawer

dread
dreaded

dream
dreamed
dreamt

dress
dressed
dresses

dried

drift

drill

drink
drank
drunk

drive
drove

drop

drown
drowned

drugs

drum

dry

dried

duck

due (*due* tomorrow)

dull

during

dust

duty

dwarf

dye (change color)

E

each

eager

ear

early
earlier
earliest

earn

earth

earthquake

ease
easy
easily

east
eastern

Easter

easy

eat

echo

ecology

economics

edge

edit
editor

education
educational

effect (a result)
effective

efficient

effort

egg
eggs

eight (8)

eighth

eighteen

eighty

either

elect
election

electric
electricity

element

elementary

elephant

elevate
elevated
elevation
elevator

eleven

elf
elves

eligible

eliminate

else

e-mail

embargo

embarrass
embarrassing
embarrassment

embrace

emerge

emergency

emit
emitted

emotional
emotionally

empathize

empire

employed
employment

empty

enable

enclose

encounter

encourage
encouragement
encouraging

encyclopedia

end

endangered

enemy
enemies

energy
energetic
energized

enforce

engage
engaged
engagement

engine
engineer

English

enjoy
enjoyed

enormous

enough

enter

entertain
entertaining
entertainment

enthusiasm
enthusiastic

entire
entirely

entitled

entrance

envelope

environment
environmentalist

equal
equally

equip
equipped
equipment

erase

erect
erected

errand

error

erupt

escape

especially

essential

establish

estimate
estimation

eternity

ethical

Europe

evaporate

even

evening

event
events

eventually

ever

evergreen

every

everybody

everyone

everything

everywhere

evidence

evolution

exactly

exaggerate
exaggeration

examine
examination
exam

example

exceed

excellent

except
exception
exceptional

exchange

excite
excited
excitement
exciting

exclaim
exclamation
exclaimed

exclusive

excuse

execution

executive

exercise

exert
exertion

exhaust
exhausted
exhausting

excerpt

exhibit
exhibition

exhilarate
exhilarated

exist
existence

exit

expand

expect
expectation

expedition

expense
expensive

experience

experiment

expert

explain
explanation

explode
exploded
explosion

explore
exploration

export

express
expression

extend

extensive

extra

extracted

extraordinary

extreme
extremely

eye
eyes

F

fabulous

face

fact

factory

fade

fail
failure

faint

fair (not *fair*/county *fair*)

faith

fall
fell

false

fame
famous

familiar

family

famous

fan

fantastic
fantasy

far

fare (bus *fare*)

farewell

farm
farmer

farther

fascinate
fascinating

fashion

fast

fasten

fat

fate

father

fault

favor
favorite

fear

feast

feather

feature

February
Feb.

feed
fed

feel
feeling
felt

feet

fell

fellow

felt

female
feminine

fence

fern

ferocious

fertile

festival

fetch

fever

few

fiction
fictitious

field

fierce
fiercely

fifteen

fifth

fifty

fight
fought

figure

file

fill

filter

final
finally

finances
financial

find
found

fine

finger

finished

fir

fire
fired

fireplace

fireworks

firm

first

fish
fishing

fit

five

fix

flag

flame

flash

flashlight

flat

flavor

flea (bug)

flee
fled (escape)

flesh

flew
fly

flexible

flies
flight

float

flock

flood

floor

flour (for baking)

flow

flower (the plant)

flu

fly
flew
flies

focused

fog

fold

folks

follow

fond

food

fool
foolish

foot

football

footsteps

for (*for* you)

forbidden

force

foreign

forest

forever

forget
forgot
forgotten

forgive

fork

form

fort

forth (go *forth*)

fortune
fortunate

forty

forward

foul (ball)

foundation

found
find

fought
fight

fountain

four (4)

fourteen

fourth (4th)

fowl (birds)

fox

fracture

fragrance

frame

frantic

free
freedom

freeze
froze
frozen

freight

French

frequent
frequently

fresh

Friday

fried

friend
friendly
friendship

fright
frightened

frog

from

front

frontier

frost

frozen

fruit

frustrated

fry
fried
frying

fuel

full

fun
funny

funds

funeral

fur

furious

furnace

furnish

furniture

further

future

G

gain

gallery

gallon

game

gang

garage

garden
gardener

gas
gasoline

gate

gather

gave

give

gaze

geese

gem

gender

general
generally

generate

generation

generous

genetic

genius

gentle

genuine

geography

German

germs

gesture

get
getting
got
gotten

ghost

giant

gift

gigantic

ginger

gingerbread

giraffe

girl

give
gave
given
giving

glacier

glad

glance

glare

glass
glasses

gleaming

glide
glided

glimpse

glistening

globe

gloomy

glory
glorious

glove
gloves

glow

glue

gnaw

go
goes
going

goal

goat

God
god
goddess

going

gold

golf

gone

good
goodness

good-bye

goose

gorgeous

got
gotten

govern
government
governor

grab
grabbed

graceful
gracefully

grade

gradual
gradually

graduate
graduation

grain

grammar

grandfather
grandpa

grandmother
grandma

granite

granted

grapefruit

grapes

graph

grass

grate (to shred)

grateful

grave

gravity

gray

grazing

grease

great (wonderful)

greed
greedy

green

greenhouse

greet
greeted

grew

grief
grieve

grind

grip

groan

grocery

ground

group

grove

grow
grew
growing

growl

grown-up

guarantee

guard

guess
guessed

guest

guide

guilt
guilty

guitar

gulf

gullible

gum

gun

gutter

guy

gym
gymnasium

H

habit

habitat

had
has

hail

hair (on your head)

half
halves

hall (*hall*way)

Halloween

halves

ham

hamburger

hammer

hand

handicap
handicapped

handkerchief

handle

handsome

handy

hang
hanged
hung

Hanukkah
Chanukah

happen
happened

happy
happiness

harbor

hard

hardly

hardships

hare (rabbit)

harm
harmful
harmless

harness

harp

harass
harassment

harsh

harvest

has
had

hat

hatch

hate
hatred

hat
hats

haul (to carry)

haunted

have
haven't
having

hawk

hay (*hay*stack)

he

head

headache

heal (to make well)

health

hear (listen)
heard

heart

heat

heaven

heavy

heel (of your foot)

height

heir (*heir* to the throne)

held
hold

hello

helmet

help
helped
helpful
helpless

hemisphere

hen

her

herd (*herd* of cattle)

here (over *here*)

hero
heroes

herself

hesitate
hesitant
hesitation

hey (*hey*, you)

hide

high
higher (*higher* up)
highest

high school

highway

hike

hill

hillside

him

himself

Hindi

Hindu
Hinduism

hinge

hire (to give someone a job)

his

Hispanic

historical

history

hit

hoarse (voice is *hoarse*)

hobby

hockey

hoe

hog

hold
held

hole (in the ground)

holiday

hollow

holy

home

homework

honest

honey

honor

hook

hop

hope
hoping
hopefully

horizon

horn

horror
horrible
horrific
horrifying

horse (the animal)

horseback

hospital

host
hostess

hot

hot dogs

hotel

hound

hour (in one *hour*)

house

household

hover

how

however

howl
howling

huddle

hug

huge

hum

human

humid
humidity

humiliate
humiliating
humiliation

humor
humorous

hundred

hung

hungry

hunt
hunting

hurry

hurt

husband

hut

hypnotize

hypocrite
hypocritical

hypothesis

I

I
I'd
I'll
I'm
I've

ice

ice cream

I'd

idea

ideal

identify

idle (not busy)

idol (a worshipped
thing or person)

if

ignorance

ignore

I'll

ill

illuminate

illustrate
illustration

I'm

image

imagine
imaginative
imagination

imitate

immature

immediate
immediately

immense

immigrant
immigrate

impact

impatient

impersonal

import

important

impossible

impression
impressive

improve
improvement

impulse

in

inauguration

inch
inches

incident

include
including

inconsiderate

inconvenience
inconvenient

incorporate

incorrect

increase

incredible
incredibly

indebted

indeed

independence
independent

indicate

individual

indoor

indulge

industry

inevitable

inexpensive

infection

inferior

infinite

influence
influential

inform
information
informative

ingenious

ingredients

inhabitants

initial

injure
injured
injury

injustice

ink

inn (a hotel)

inattentive

inner

innocent

innumerable

inquire

insect

inseparable

inside

insist
insistent

inspect

inspire
inspiration
inspired

install

instance

instant
instantly

instead

instruct
instructor
instruction

instrument

insult
insulting

insure
insurance

integrate
integration

intellectual

intelligence
intelligent

intended

intense

intent
intention

interest
interesting

interfere

interior

international

Internet

interpret
interpreter

interrupt
interruption

interval

interview

intestine

into

intolerant

intricate

introduce
introduction

intrigue
intriguing

invade
invasion

invent
invention

investigate
investigation

invisible

invite
invitation

involve

iron

irony
ironic

irrelevant

irrigate

irritating

is
isn't

Islam
Islamic

island

isle (small island)

issue

it
its (hurt *its* paw)
it's (it is)

itself

I've

J

jacket

jail

jam

janitor

January
Jan.

Japanese

jar

jaw

jealous

Jewish
Judaism

jewelry

job

join

joints

joke

jolly

journal

journey

joy

judge
judicial
judgment

juice

July

jump
jumped

June

jungle

junior
Jr.

jury

just
justice

K

keep
kept

kettle

key

keyboard

kick

kid
kids

kidnap
kidnapped

kill
killed

kilometer

kind
kindness
kinds

kindergarten

kindness

king

kiss
kisses

kitchen

kite

kitten

knee

kneel

knew
know

knife
knives

knight (in shining armor)

knit

knives

knob

knock

knot (tie a knot)

know
known
knew

knowledge

Korean

Kwanza

L

label

labor

laboratory

lace

lack

lad

ladder

lady
ladies

laid

lake

lamb

lamp

land

landlord

lane

language

lap

large

lark

laser

last

late
later

latter

laugh
laughed
laughter

laundry

law
lawyer

lawn

lay

layer

lazy

lead
leader
led

leaf
leaves

league

leak

lean

leap

learn

least

leather

leave
leaves
leaving

lecture

led

left

legal

legislature

legitimate

legs

leisure

lemon

lemonade

length

less

lesson

let
let's

letter

level

liable

liberty

library

license

lick

lid

lie
lied
lying

lieutenant

life

lift

light
lit

lightning

like
liked

lily

limb

limit
limited

limp

line
lining

linen

link
linking

lion

lips

liquid

list

listen

literal
literally

literature

littered

little

live
living

load

loaf

loan

local

locate
located
location

lock
locker

locomotive

log

lonesome

long

look
looked

loop

loose

lose
lost

lot
lots

lotion

loud

love
lovely
loving

low

loyal

lumber

luck
lucky

ludicrous

lunch

lungs

lurk

luscious

lying

M

macaroni

machine

mad

made
make

magazine

magic
magician

magnificent

magnitude

mail (letters)

main (*main* idea)

Maine (state of *Maine*)

maintain
maintenance

majestic

major

majority

make
made
making

male
masculine

malicious

mammal

man

manage
manager

mane (horse's *mane*)

maneuver

manner

mansion

manual

manufacture
manufacturer

many

map

maple

marbles

March

mark

market

marry
marriage
married

marshmallows

masculine

mash

mask

mass
massive

master

masterpiece

match

mate

material

math
mathematics

matter

mature

maximum

May (the month)

may (you *may*)

maybe

mayor

me

meadow

meal

mean
meaning
meant

meantime

meanwhile

measure

meat (the food)

mechanical

medal

medical

medicine

meet (get together)
met

melt

member

memory
memorable
memories
memorize

men

mend

mental
mentally

mention

merchant

mercy
merciful

mere
merely

merry

message

met

metal

meter

method

metric

mice

microscope

middle

midnight

might

mild

mile

military

milk

mill

million
millionaire

mind

mine

mineral

miniature

minimum

minister

mink

minute

miracle
miraculous

mirror

mischief
mischievous

miserable

misfortune
misfortunate

misplace
misplaced

miss
missed

mission

mistake

misunderstand
misunderstood

mix
mixed

mock

model

moderate

modern
modernize

modify
modified

moist
moisture

mold

moment
momentarily

monarchy

Monday

money
monetary

monitor

monkey

monologue

monotone
monotonous

monstrous

month

monument
monumental

moon

mop

moral
morally

more

morning

mosque

mosquito
mosquitoes

moss

most

mother

motion

motivate
motivation

motor

mount

mountain

mouse
mice

mouth

move
moved
movement

movie

mow

Mr.

Mrs.

Ms.

much

mud

mule

multiply
multiplication

multitude

mumble

Muslim
Moslem

murder
murderer

murmur

muscles

museum

music
musician

must

my

myself

mystery
mysterious

myth
mythology

N

nail

name

napkin

narrate
narration
narrator

narrow

nation
national

native

Native American

nature
natural

naughty

nauseous
nauseating

navy

near
nearly

neat

necessary
necessarily

neck

necklace

need

needle

negative

neighbor

neighborhood

neither

nephew

nerve
nervous

nest

net

never

nevertheless

new (brand *new*)

news

newspaper

next

nice

nickel

niece

night (sleep at *night*)

nightmare

nine

nineteen

ninety

ninth

no (yes and *no*)

nobody

noise

nonchalant
nonchalantly

none (not any)

noon

no one

nor

normal
normally

north
northern

North America
North American

nose
nosy

not

note

notebook

nothing

notice

notify

noun

novel

November
Nov.

now

nowadays

nowhere

numb

number

numerous

nun (clergy)

nurse

nutrient
nutritious

nuts

O

oak

oar (use to row a boat)

oatmeal

oats

obedient
obey

object

obligated

oblivion
oblivious

obnoxious

observe
observation
observatory

obstacles

obtain

obvious
obviously

occasion
occasionally

occupy
occupation
occupied

occur
occurred
occurrence

ocean

o'clock

October
Oct.

odor

of

off

offense
offensive

offer

office
officer
official

often

oh

oil

OK
okay

old

olive

on

one
once

one half

onion

only

open

opera

operate
operation

opinion
opinionated

opponent

opportunity

opposite

optimistic

option

or (you *or* me)

oral

orange

orchard

orchestra

order

ordinary

ore (iron *ore*)

organic

organize
organization

organ

origin

original
originally

ornaments

other

ought

our (*our* house)

ourselves

out

outdoors

outline

outrageous

outside

outstanding

oven

over

overalls

overwhelming

owe (to *owe* money)

owl

own
owned

ox

oxygen

P

Pacific

pack

package

pad

paddle

page

pageant

paid

pail (a bucket)

pain (ouch!)

paint
painting

pair (two of a kind)

pajamas

palace

pale (not bright)

palm

pan

pane (window *pane*)

panic
panicked

pantry

pants

paper

parade

paradise

paragraph

paralysis
paralyze

paranoid

pardon

parents

park

part

partial

participate

particular
particularly

partner

parts

party

pass
passed

passage

passenger

passion

Passover

past (drove *past/
past* tense)

paste

pasture

pat

path

pathetic

patient
patiently

pattern

pause

pave

pavement

pay
paid

peace
peaceful
peacefully

peach

peak

peanuts

pear (fruit)

pearl

peas (vegetable)

peasant

pecan

peculiar
peculiarity

pedal (bike *pedal*)

peek (to look)

peel (banana *peel*)

peep

peer

peg

pen

pencil

penny	phase	pigs
people	phenomenal	pile
per	philosophy	pillow
percent	phone	pilot
perceive	phony	pin
perception		
	photocopy	pine
perfect		
	photograph	pineapple
perform	photography	
performance		pink
	phrase	
perfume		pioneers
	physical	
perhaps	physically	pipe
period	physical education	pirate
	phys ed	
permanent		pistol
	piano	
permit		pit
permitted	pick	
permission		pitch
	pickles	pitcher
person		
personal	picnic	pity
personality		
	picture	place
perspective		
	pie	plague
persuade		
persuasive	piece (of pie)	plain (ordinary)
pet	pierce	plan
petals	pigeon	plane (jet)

planet

plank

plant

plantation

plastic

plate

platform

play
played
playing

playground

pleasant

please

pleasure
pleasurable

pledge

plenty

plot

plow

plum

plumber

plunge

plural

plus

pocket

pocketbook

poem
poet
poetry

point

poison
poisonous

poke

polar

pole

police

policy

Polish (a language)

polish (to shine)
polished

polite

politics
political
politician

pollute
pollution

pond

pony

pool

poor (not rich)

pop

popcorn

popular

population

porch

pore (in your skin)

pork

port

portfolio

portion

Portuguese

position

positive
positively

possess
possessed
possession

possible
possibly

post

post office

pot

potato
potatoes

potential
potentially

poultry

pound

pour (a drink)

poverty

powder

power
powerful

practical
practically

practice
practicing

prairie

pray
prayer

preach

precarious
precariously

precede
preceded

precious

predict
predictable

prefer
preference

perform
performers

prejudice

prepare
preparation

preposition

presence

present
presentation

preserve

president

press

pressure

presume

pretend

pretty

prevail

prevent

preview

previous
previously

prey (stalks its *prey*)

price

priest

primary
primarily

prime

primitive

prince
princess

principal (head of a
    school)

principle (a rule)

print
printer

prison

private
privacy

privilege
privileged

prize

probably

problem

procedure
proceed

process

produce

product
productive

profession
professional

professor

profit

program

progress

project
projector

prominent

promise

promote
promotion

pronoun

pronounce
pronunciation

proof
prove

propeller

proper

property

propose
proposal

prosper

protect
protection
protective

protein

Protestant

protest

proud

prove
proven

provide

province

P.S.

psychology
psychological
psychologist

public
publicity

publish

pudding

pull
pulled

pulp

pump

pumpkin

punish
punishment

pup
puppy

pupil
pupils

purchase

pure

purple

purpose
purposely

purse

pursue
pursued

push
pushed

put
putting

puzzle

pyramids

Q

quality

quantity

quarrel

quart

quarter

queen

queer

query

question

quick
quickly

quiet

quilt

quit

quite

quiz

quotation

quote

R

rabbit

race
racism

rack

racket (a noise)

racquet (for tennis)

radiate
radiant
radiator

radio

raft

rag
ragged

rail

railroad

rain
raining

rainbow

rainfall

rain forest

raise

rake

ran

ranch

range

rank

rap (music/to tap)

rapid
rapidly

rare
rarely

rat

rate

rather

rattle

raw

reach
reached

react
reaction

read
reading

ready

real
realistic
reality

realize
realized

really

rear

reason
reasonable

rebel

recall
recalled

receive
received
receipt

recent
recently

recess

reckless
recklessly

recognize
recognition

recommend
recommendation

record

recover
recovery

recreation

red (the color)

reduce
reduction

refer
referred
reference

refine
refining

reflect
reflecting
reflection

refresh
refreshing

refuse

regard
regarding
regards

region
regional

register
registration

regret

regular
regularly

rehearse
rehearsal

reign (rule)

reindeer

reins (on a horse)

reject

rejoice

relate
relations

relationship

relax

release

relevant

relieve
relieved
relief

religion
religious

reluctant
reluctance
reluctantly

remain

remark
remarkable

remember

remind
reminder

reminisce
reminiscent

remove
removal

renew
renewal

rent
rental

repair

repeat
repetition

reply
replied

report

represent
representation
representative

reptile

republic
Republican

request

require
requirement

rescue

research

resemble

reserve
reservation

reservoir

reside
residence

resign
resignation

resist
resistance

resolve

resort

resource
resourceful
resources

respect
respectfully

respond
response

responsible
responsibility

rest

restaurant

result

resume

retired

retrieve

return

reveal

review

revise
revision

revolution
revolutionary

reward

rhyme

rhythm

ribbon

rice

rich

rid

ride
riding
rode

ridiculous

right (correct)

rim

ring
rang
rung

rinse

ripe

rise
risen
rose

rival

river

road (street)

roam

roast

robin

robot

rock

rocket

rod

role (part in a play)

roll
rolled

rollerblades

romantic

roof

room

root (of a tree)

rope

rose

rot
rotten

rough

round

route (paper *route*)

routine

row

royal

rub

rubber

rubbish

rude

rug

ruin

rule
ruler

rumor

run
running

rural

rush

Russian

rust

S

sack

sacrifice

sad

saddle

safe

said

sail (*sail* a boat)

salad

salary

sale (for *sale*)

salesperson

salmon

salt

salute

same

sand

sandwich

sang

sarcastic
sarcastically

sat

satisfy
satisfied
satisfying

satisfaction
satisfactory

Saturday

sauce

save

saw

say
said

scale

scarce

scare
scared
scary

scarf

scarlet

scattered

scene
scenery

scent (a smell)

schedule

scheme

scholar
scholarly

school

science
scientific
scientist

scissors

scold

score

scout

scrap

scrape

scratch

scream

screen

screw

scribble

scrub

scrumptious

sculpt
sculpture

scurry
scurries
scurrying

sea (ocean)

seal

seam (of a dress)

seaport

search

season

seat

second

secret
secretly

secretary

section

secure
security

see
saw
seen

seed

seek

seem (to *seem* upset)

seen (I've *seen* it.)

seize

seldom

select
selection
selective

self
selfish

sell

semester

senate
senator

send
sent

senior

sensation
sensational

sense (common *sense*)

senseless
senselessly

sensible

sensitive

sentence

separate
separately
separation

September
Sept.

sequel

serene

series

serious
seriously

serve
service

session

set

settle
settling

seven

seventh

seventy

several

severe
severely

seventeen

sew
sewed
sewing

sewage
sewer

shack

shade
shadow

shake

shall (I *shall* go.)

shallow

shape

share

shark

sharp

shave

she

shear (to cut)
shears

shed

sheep

sheer (transparent)

sheet

shelf

shell (seashell)

shelter

shepherd

shine
shined
shining

shingle

ship

shipment

shirt

shiver

shock
shocking

shoe

shoot

shop
shopping

shore

short

shot

should

shoulder

shout

shove

shovel

show
showed
shown

shower

shriek

shrimp

shrubs
shrubbery

shut

shy

sibling

sick
sickening

side

sidewalk

sigh
sighed

sight (eye*sight*)

sign

signal

signature

significance
significant

silence
silent

silk

silly

silver

similar
similarity

simple

simultaneous
simultaneously

since

sincerely

sing
sang
sung

single

sink

sir

sister

sit

site (a location)

sitting

situation

six

sixteen

sixth

sixty

size

skate
skating

skateboard

skeleton

ski
skiing
skis

skin

skip

skirt

skunk

sky
skies

slam

slant

slave
slavery

sled
sledding

sleep
slept

sleeve
sleigh (sled)

slept

slice

slide

slight

slime
slimy

slip
slippery

slippers

solemn

slow

small

smart

smell
smelled
smelt

smile
smiling

smoke
smoking

smooth

snake

snap

snatch

sneak
sneaked

sneeze

snicker

snow
snowed
snowing

snowboard

snowman

so

soak

soap

soar (to fly)

soccer

social

social studies

society

socks

soda

soft
soften

soil

sold

soldier

sole (of a shoe)

solemn
solemnly

solid

solve

solution

some (*some* people)

somebody

someday

someone

something

sometimes

somewhere

son (and daughter)

song

soon

soothe
soothing

sophisticated
sophistication

sore (*sore* throat)

sorrow

sorry

sort

soul (spirit)
soulful

sound

soup

sour

source

south
southern

South America
South American

souvenir

space
spacious

spaghetti

Spanish

spare

spark
sparkling

speak
spoke
spoken

speech

special

species

specific
specifically

spectacle
spectacular

speculate
speculation

speech

speed
sped

spell
spelling

spend
spent

spices

spider

spill

spin

spinach

spirit
spiritual

spite

splash

splendid

split

spoil

spoke

sponge

spoon

sport
sports

sponge

spot

sprained

spray

spread

spring

sprinkle

sprout

spy
spying

square

squeak
squeaking
squeaky

squeal
squealed

squeeze

squirrel

stable

stack

stadium

stage

stain

stairs

stake (a stick)

stalk

stall

stamp
stamps

stand
stood

standard

star

starch

stare
stared
staring

start
started

startled

state

statement

station
stationary (still)

stationery (paper)

statue

stay
stayed
staying

steady

steak (a food)

steal
stole
stolen

steam

steel (metal)

steep

steer

stem

stench

step
stepped

stepfather

stepmother

stereotype

stick

stiff

still

stir
stirred

stitch

stockings

stole

stomach

stomachache

stone

stood

stool

stoop

stop
stopped

store

storm

story
stories

stove

straight
straightened

strain

strange
stranger

strap

straw

streak

stream

street

streetcar

strength
strengthen

stretch
stretched
stretching

strike

string

stripe

stroke

stroll

strong

struck

structure

struggle
struggling

stubborn

stuck

student

study
studying

stuff

stumble

stun
stunned
stunning

stunt

style
stylish

subject
subjected

subscribe
subscription

substitute

subtle
subtly

subtract

subway

succeed
succeeded

success
successful
successfully

such

suck

sudden
suddenly

sue
sueing

suffer

sufficient

sugar

suggest
suggested
suggestion

suicide

suit

sullen

sum (the total)

summary
summarize

summer

sun (a star)

Sunday

sunset

sunshine

super

superintendent

superior

superlative

superstition

supper

supply

support

suppose
supposed

supreme

sure
surely

surface

surprise
surprised

surround
surrounded
surroundings

survive
survival

suspense
suspenseful

suspicious
suspicion
suspiciously

swallow

swamp

sway

sweat
sweater

sweep

sweet

swift

swim
swam
swimming
swum

swing

switch

sword

symbolic
symbolize

sympathy
symphathize
sympathetic

symphony

system
systematic
systematically

T

table

tablet

tack
tacks (pins)

tag

tail (*tail* on the donkey)

take
taking

took

tale (fairy *tale*)

talent
talented

talk
talked

tall

tame

tan

tank

tap

task

taste

taught

tax
taxes

taxi
taxis

tea

teach
teacher
teaches
taught

teacup

team

tear
tore
torn

tease

teaspoon
tsp.

technical
technically

technique

technology
technological

teenage
teenager

teeth
tooth

telephone

telescope

television

tell
told

temperature

temple

temporary
temporarily

ten

tender

tennis

tension

tent

tentatively

tenth

term

terrible
terribly

terrific

terrify
terrifying

territory
territorial

terror
terrorism
terrorist

test

testimony

text

textbook

than (more *than*)

thank

Thanksgiving

that
that's

thaw

the

theater

their (*their* house)

them

themselves

then (now and *then*)

theory
theoretical
theoretically

there
there's

therefore

these

they
they're

thick

thief
thieves

thin

thing

think
thinking

third

thirst
thirsty

thirteen

thirty

this

thorough
thoroughly

those

though

thought

thousand

thread

threat
threaten

three

threw
throw

thrift
thrifty

thrill
thrilling

throat

throne (the king's)

through (*through* with
  dinner)

throughout

throw
threw
thrown

thumb

thump

thunder

Thursday

thus

ticket

tide (ocean *tide*)

tie
tied
tying

tiger

tight

till

time
timer

tin

tinsel

tiny

tip

tire
tired

tissue

title
titled

to (*to* the store)

toad

toast

today

toe (on your foot)

together

toilet

told

tolerant
tolerance

tomato
tomatoes

tomb

tomorrow

ton

tone
toning

tongue

tonight

tonsil

too (me *too*)

tool

tooth
teeth

top

topic

torch

tore
torn

toss

total
totally

touch

tough

tour
tourist

tournament

tow (a car)
towing

toward
towards

towel

town

toxic
toxin

toy
toys

track

tractor

trade

tradition
traditional

traffic

tragic
tragedy

trail

train

traitor

tramp

tranquil

transform
transformation

transport
transportation

trap
trapped

trash

travel
traveler

tray

treacherous
treachery

treasure

treat

trees

trek

trembling

tremendous

triangle
triangular

tribe

trick

tried

trigger

trip

triple

triumph

troops

tropics
tropical

trouble
troubling

truck

true
truly
truth

trumpets

trunk

trust

truth

try
tried
trying

tube

Tuesday

tug

tumble

tune

tunnel

turf

turkey

turmoil

turn

turnpike

turtle

twelfth

twelve

twenty

twice

twin

twine

two

type

typewriter

typical

U

ugly

ultimate

umbrella

umpire

unable

unacceptable

unanimous

unbelievable

uncertain

uncle

uncomfortable

uncommon

unconscious

uncontrollable

unconventional

undecided

under

underground

underneath

understand
understandable
understood

unexpected
unexpectedly

unfair

unfamiliar

unforgettable

unfortunate
unfortunately

unhappy

uniform

union

unique

unit

unite
united

United States of
   America (U.S.A)

university

unknown

unless

unload

unnatural

unpleasant

unsatisfactory

unselfish
unselfishly

unsuccessful
unsuccessfully

unsuspecting

until

unusual

unwanted

up

upon

upset

upstairs

urge

urgent

us

usable

use
used

useful

useless

usual
usually

V

vacancy
vacant

vacation

vaccine

vacuum

vague

vain (conceited)

valentine

valid
validate

valley

value
valuable
values

vane (weather *vane*)

vanilla

vanish

vapor

variables
variety
various

vase

vast

vat

vegetables

vehemently

vehicle

vein (carries blood)

verb

verse

version

very

vessel

veteran

veto
vetoes

vibrant
vibrancy

vice president

vicinity

victim

victory
victorious

video

videotape

Vietnamese

view

village

villain

vine

vinegar

violate
violation

violent
violence

violet

virus

visible
vision

visit
visitor

vitamin

vocabulary

vocation

voice

volcano
volcanoes

volleyball

volume

volunteer

vote
voting

voyage

vulnerable

W

wade

wage

wagon

waist (a body part)

wait
waiter
waitress

wake
woke

walk

wall

walnut

wander
wandering

want
wanted
wants

war (battle)

warehouse

warm
warmth

warn
warning

warrant

was
wasn't

wash
washed
washer

waste (a *waste* of time)

watch

water

waterfall

watermelon

wave

wax

way (which *way*?)

we
we'll
we're
we've

weak (not strong)

wealth
wealthy

weapon

wear
wore
worn

weather
weathered

weave
weaving

web

World Wide Web
Web site

wedding

Wednesday

weed
weeding

week (7 days)

weep

weigh
weight

weird

welcome

welfare

we'll

well

went

we're

were

west

wet

we've

whale

wharf

what

whatever

wheat

wheel

when

where (*Where* are you?)

wherever

whether (*whether* or
    not)

which (*Which* one?)

while

whine (complain)

whip

whirl
whirled

whisper

whistle

white

who
who's (*who is*)

whose (*Whose* book
    is this?)

whole (the *whole* thing)

wholesome

whom

who's (*who is*)

whose (*whose* book)

why

wide
width

wife
wives

wild

wilderness

will
won't

willow

win
won

wind
windy

windmill

window

wing
wings
winged

winner

winter

wipe

wire
wireless

wise

wish
wished

witch (*witch's* brew)

with

within

without

wizard

woke

warewolf

wolves

woman
women

won (the game)

wonder
wonderful

won't

wood
wooden
woods

wool
woolen

word

wore (*wore* a costume)

work

world

worm

worn (*worn* out)

worry
worried
worrying

worse
worst

worth

would
wouldn't

wound
wounded

wrap
wrapped
wrapper

wreath

wreck

wrestle
wrestling

wring (to twist)

wrinkle
wrinkly

wrist

write
writer
writing
written
wrote

wrong

X

Xerox

xylophone

Y

yacht

yard

yarn

yawn

yeah

year

yeast

yell
yelled

yellow

yes

yesterday

yet

yield

yolk

you
you'd

you'll

your (*your* dog)
yours

you're (*you are*)

young

yourself

youth
youthful

Z

zebra

zero

zone

zoo
zoologist
zoology

DICTIONARY

Homonyms,

Homophones, and Words Commonly Confused

HOMONYMS

Homonyms,

Homophones,
and Words Commonly Confused

accept (*accept* a gift)
except (everyone *except* me)

affect (to change or influence)
effect (a result)

air (what we breathe)
heir (*heir* to the throne)

aisle (in a movie theater)
isle (small island)

ant (small insect)
aunt (*Aunt* Sue)

ate (*ate* a meal)
eight (8)

bare (to show; exposed)
bear (an animal)

berry (a fruit)
bury (to place in the ground)

blew (*blew* out the candles)
blue (a color)

boar (wild pig)
boor (a rude person)
bore (to drill; to put someone to
  sleep; a boring person)

board (plank of wood)
bored (not interested)

bough (branch)
bow (take a *bow*)

brake (in a car)
break (to destroy something)

buy (in a store)
by (*by* 5:00; built by many workers)
bye (good-*bye*)

capital (*capital* letter; *capital* city)
capitol (building where legislature
  meets)

cent (¢)
scent (odor)
sent (*sent* a letter)

cents (5¢)
sense (common *sense*)

chews (eats)
choose (*choose* a seat)

coarse (rough)
course (a class; a path)

creak (a noise)
creek (a brook)

dear (*Dear* Jeffrey)
deer (an animal)

desert (the Sahara)
dessert (ice cream, cake)

dew (moisture)
do (I *do*.)
due (*due* tomorrow)

doe (female deer)
dough (unbaked bread)

die (live and *die*)
dye (change color)

eye (what we see with)
I (me)

fair (*fair* treatment; county *fair*)
fare (bus *fare*)

fir (a tree)
fur (animal *fur*)

flea (a bug)
flee (to escape)

flew (*flew* away)
flu (*flu* shot)
flue (chimney *flue*)

flour (for baking)
flower (a daisy)

for (out *for* lunch)
fore (The golfer yells, *"fore!"*)
four (4)

forth (go *forth*)
fourth (4th)

foul (*foul* ball; *foul* smell)
fowl (type of bird)

grate (to shred)
great (wonderful)

guessed (drew a conclusion)
guest (a visitor)

hair (on your head)
hare (rabbit)

hall (entranceway)
haul (to carry)

hay (*hay*ride)
hey (*hey*, you)

heal (to cure)
heel (on a foot)

hear (*hear* a voice)
here (*here* it is)

heard (*heard* a noise)
herd (*herd* of deer)

higher (*higher* up)
hire (*hire* a plumber)

him (a boy or man)
hymn (a song)

hoarse (a *hoarse* voice)
horse (an animal)

hole (a deep *hole*)
whole (the *whole* thing)

HOMONYMS

in (*in* and out)
inn (stay at the *inn*)

its (possession: *its* paw)
it's (contraction: *it is*)

knew (*knew* the answer)
new (brand *new*)

know (*know* the answer)
no (*no* thank you)

loose (dog is *loose*)
lose (*lose* your wallet)

made (*made* by hand)
maid (young girl or worker)

mail (a letter or package)
male (a boy or man)

main (the *main* idea)
Maine (state of *Maine*)
mane (a horse's *mane*)

meat (beef)
meet (to get together)

missed (I *missed* you.)
mist (vapor)

morning (a.m.)
mourning (grieving)

night (p.m.)
knight (in shining armor)

none (zero)
nun (religious worker)

not (*not* today)
knot (*knot* in my shoelace)

or (you *or* me)
oar (for rowing a boat)
ore (a mineral)

one (1)
won (*won* the game)

our (*our* house)
are (we *are*)

hour (60 minutes)

oh (*oh* no!)
owe (*owe* money)

pail (a bucket)
pale (not bright)

pain (ouch!)
pane (in a window)

pair (two)
pare (to peel)
pear (a fruit)

passed (*passed* the salt)
past (*past*, present, future)

peace (*peace* on earth)
piece (a *piece* of pie)

plain (ordinary)
plane (aircraft)

poor (not rich)
pore over (to study carefully)
pour (*pour* a drink)

pray (*pray* for rain)
prey (stalk its *prey*)

rain (precipitation)
reign (rule or government)
rein (a strap; guiding power)

read (*read* a book)
red (the color)

read (to *read* a book)
reed (wooden mouthpiece; blade of
  grass)

right (*right* and left; *right* and wrong)
write (*write* a story)

ring (diamond *ring*)
wring (*wring* out a towel)

road (45 Oak *Road*)
rode (*rode* a bike)

role (a part in a play)
roll (to push a ball; a biscuit)

root (*root* of a tree)
route (a paper *route*)

sail (*sail* a boat)
sale (clearance *sale*)

scene (Act I, *scene* 2)
seen (Have you *seen* her?)

sea (an ocean)
see (to view)

seam (of a dress)
seem (appear)

sell (*sell* your car)
cell (plant *cell*; prison *cell*)

sew (with needle and thread)
so (*So* what?)

shall (*shall* be finished soon)
shell (sea*shell*)

sight (out of *sight*)
site (Web *site*)

slay (to kill)
sleigh (a horse-drawn vehicle)

soar (to fly)
sore (injured)

sole (the bottom of a shoe; a kind
  of fish)
soul (a spirit; a person)

some (*some* of us)
sum (the total)

son (*son* or daughter)
sun (*sun* and moon)

stair (climb the *stair*)
stare (*stare* at someone)

stationary (not moving)
stationery (papers, envelopes, etc.)

stake (a stick)
steak (meat)

steal (to take something)
steel (a strong metal)

suite (the honeymoon *suite*)
sweet (*sweet* potatoes)

sure (certain)
shore (the coast)

tacks (pins)
tax (money)

tail (a dog's *tail*)
tale (a fairy *tale*)

taught (trained)
taut (tight)
tot (a young child)

tea (*tea* or coffee)
tee (a golf *tee*)

than (more *than* five)
then (now and *then*)

there (*There* you are.)
their (possession: *their* house)
they're (contraction: *they are*)

thorough (a *thorough* examination)
throw (*throw* that out)

threw (*threw* a party)
through (*through* with dinner; *through* the door)

throne (the king's *throne*)
thrown (The ball was *thrown*.)

tide (high *tide*, low *tide*)
tied (*tied* his laces)

to (*to* run; *to* the store)
too (me *too*; *too* many)
two (2)

toe (fingers and *toes*)
tow (*tow* truck)

told (*told* me the truth)
tolled (The bell *tolled*.)

tore (*tore* her sweater)
tour (*tour* the museum)

vain (conceited)
vane (a moveable device)
vein (carries blood)

waist (size 36 *waist*)
waste (to *waste* your time)

war (wage a *war*)
wore (*wore* glasses)

warn (*warn* him of danger)
worn (*worn* out)

wait (*Wait* until later.)
weight (height and *weight*)

way (Which *way* do we go?)
weigh (How much does this *weigh*?)

well (not feeling *well*)
we'll (contraction: *we will*)
wheel (*wheel* of a car)

were (We *were* there.)
we're (contraction: *we are*)

wear (*wear* a coat)
where (who, what, *where*)

weave (*weave* a basket)
we've (contraction: *we have*)

weak (not strong)
week (seven days)

weather (*weather* forecast)
whether (*whether* or not)

which (*which* way)
witch (*witch's* brew)

who's (contraction: *who is*)
whose (possession: *whose* book)

woman (one adult female)
women (two or more adult females)

wood (*wood* table)
would (*Would* you help me?)

wrap (*wrap* a present)
rap (*rap* on the door; *rap* music)

your (possession: *your* room)
you're (contraction: *you are*)

HOMONYMS

Thesaurus

Words to Use When You Write . . .

Words to Use When You Write Transitions

a few minutes later	however	similarly
a moment later	in addition	sometimes
a while later	in conclusion	soon
accordingly	in contrast	still
additionally	in spite of	subsequently
after that	in spite of this	therefore
afterward	in sum	though
again	in summary	to sum up
also	in that case	to summarize
although	in the same way	unlike
another difference	instead	yet
another point to keep in mind	later	
another reason	like	
as a result	likewise	
at that moment	more importantly	
at this point	moreover	
but	most important	
consequently	nevertheless	
despite	next	
even though	nonetheless	
eventually	now	
finally	on the contrary	
first	on the other hand	
first of all	once more	
following that	recently	
for all these reasons	regardless	
for example	second	
for instance	secondly	
furthermore	shortly after that	
	similar to	

Words to Use When You Write about Literature

abstract poetry	culture	legend
adventure	descriptive	literary device
allegory	detective	memoir
alliteration	device	metaphor
allusion	diary	meter
anecdote	drama	motif
antagonist	epic	myth
anthology	episode	narrative
antithesis	essay	nonfiction
archetype	exposition	novel
assonance	fairy tale	novella
author	fantasy	ode
autobiography	farce	omniscient
ballad	fiction	parody
biography	first-person	playwright
blank verse	flashback	plot
canon	foil	poem, poetry
characterization	folk tale	poetic license
cliché	free verse	point of view
climax	genre	preface
comedy	Gothic	prose
compare	haiku	protagonist
conclusion	historical novel	realism
conflict	horror	Renaissance
contemporary	hyperbole	review
contrast	imagery	rhyme
criticism	irony	rhythm
critique	journal	romance

THESAURUS

satire

scansion

science fiction

Shakespeare

short story

simile

soliloquy

sonnet

stanza

story

symbolism

the classics

thesis

third-person

tragedy

utopia

verse

Victorian

vignette

voice

Words to Use When You Write about Social Studies

abolitionist

aborigine

agriculture

amendment

apartheid

archipelago

article

artifact

assimilation

ballot

Bill of Rights

bipartisan

boycott

budget

Cabinet

campaign

canal

capital

capitalism

Capitol

caste

census

checks and balances

citizen

citizenship

city

Civil War

civilization

class

climate

cold war

colonialism

colony

commonwealth

communism

Congress

Constitution

continent

crop

culture

custom

Declaration of
   Independence

deficit

democracy

Democrat

demography

depression

desegregation

desert

dictatorship

economics

election

emancipate

embargo

emigrate

empire

employment

equator

erosion

ethnocentrism

executive branch

extended family

famine

federal

feminism

freedom

glacier

government

governor

gulf

harbor

hemisphere

Holocaust

House of
   Representatives

human rights

impeach

inauguration

independence

indigenous

Industrial Revolution

inflation

irrigation

isthmus

judicial branch

labor

landform

latitude

legislative branch

liberty

lobbyist

longitude

matriarchy

mayor

melting pot

migration

military

monarchy

monopoly

mountain

nation

natural resource

naturalize

neighborhood

nomination

nuclear family

oasis

ocean

pardon

parliament

patriarchy

patriotism

peninsula

plain

plateau

pluralism

policy

poll

population

poverty

precipitation

prejudice

president

prime meridian

prime minister

recession

refugee

religious tolerance

representative

republic

Republican

reservation

Revolutionary War

ritual

river

rural

salary

secede

Senate

sharecropper

slavery

social security

socialism

solidarity

Speaker of the House

steppe

strike

subsistence farmer

suburban

suffrage

Supreme Court

surplus

taxation

terrorism

treaty

tribe

tributary

trust

tundra

Underground Railroad

union

United Nations

urban

veto

Vice President

vote

_____

_____

_____

_____

_____

_____

acceleration

acid

alloy

amino acid

amoeba

artery

asbstract

astronomy

atmosphere

atom

bacteria

balance

barometer

base

beaker

biodegradable

biology

biome

bond

calorie

carbohydrate

carbon

carbon cycle

carbon dioxide

carnivore

catalyst

cell

Celsius

centrifuge

chemistry

chlorophyll

chromosome

clone

compound

conductor

consumer

control

cytoplasm

data

decomposer

density

dew point

digestion

DNA

Earth

earth science

earthquake

eclipse

ecology

electricity

electron

element

embryo

endangered species

energy

environment

enzyme

equilibrium

evaporation

evidence

evolution

excretion

experiment

Fahrenheit

fission

formula

fossil

frequency

friction

fusion

gas

gene

genetics

glucose

gravity

greenhouse effect

habitat

half-life

herbivore

hypothesis

inertia

invertebrate

ion

Jupiter

THESAURUS

Kelvin

kinetic

laser

lipid

liquid

magnet

mammal

Mars

mass

matter

meiosis

Mercury

metabolism

meteor

metric system

microscope

mitosis

molecule

momentum

mutation

Neptune

neutron

nucleus

observation

omnivore

orbit

organism

osmosis

oxygen

ozone layer

particle

periodic table

petri dish

pH

phase

photosynthesis

physics

Pluto

polarity

pollution

predator

producer

protein

proton

radiation

rain forest

ray

recycling

reptile

research

respiration

result

RNA

satellite

Saturn

scavenger

scientific method

solid

solution

species

spectrum

test tube

thermometer

Uranus

vacuum

variables

vein

velocity

Venus

volt

watt

weight

zenith

Words to Use When You Write about Math

addition	geometry	radical
algebra	graph	radius
angle	hypotenuse	range
area	integer	ratio
arithmetic	intersection	right angle
average	line	set
axis	mean	square root
binomial	median	statistics
calculator	mode	subtraction
circumference	multiple	sum
coefficient	multiplication	variable
compass	numerator	volume
congruent	parallel	
constant	percent	
coordinates	perimeter	
decimal	permutation	
degree	perpendicular	
denominator	pi (π)	
diagonal	place value	
diameter	point	
difference	polygon	
digit	prime number	
division	prism	
equation	probability	
estimate	product	
exponent	proportion	
factor	protractor	
fraction	quotient	

Words to Use When You Write about Music

Instruments

bagpipe

banjo

bass drum

bassoon

bongo

brass

bugle

castanets

cello

clarinet

clave

cymbals

English horn

flute

French horn

glockenspiel

guitar

harmonica

harp

kazoo

kettle drum

keyboard

oboe

percussion

piano

piccolo

recorder

saxophone

shofar

sitar

snare drum

steel drum

string

tambourine

triangle

trombone

tuba

tympanum

viola

violin

wind

woodwind

xylophone

Genres

alternative

blues

classical

country

disco

electronic

elevator

folk

funk

hard rock

heavy metal

hip-hop

house

jazz

Latin

Motown

New Age

New Wave

opera

pop

protest

punk

R&B

rap

rave

reggae

ska

soul

swing

techno

Words to Use When You Write about Art

abstract

acrylic

avant-garde

batik

brush

canvas

cartoon

charcoal

cubism

decoupage

digital

drawing

easel

expressionism

fresco

graphic art

Impressionism

illustration

landscape

medium

minimal

modernism

mural

naturalism

oil paint

palette

papier-mâché

pastel

perspective

photography

plaster

pop art

portrait

proportion

realism

Renaissance

scratchboard

sculpture

self-portrait

still life

surrealism

watercolor

Big

astronomical, broad, bulky, colossal, considerable, enormous, gargantuan, giant, gigantic, grand, great, huge, immense, important, inflated, jumbo, large, mammoth, massive, mega, mighty, monstrous, mountainous, overgrown, roomy, spacious, substantial, thundering, tremendous, vast, wide

Small

compact, dainty, diminutive, fragile, insignificant, meager, microscopic, miniature, minuscule, minute, petty, puny, scant, tiny, unimportant, weak, wee

Very

awfully, exceedingly, exceptionally, extremely, fairly, intensely, mightily, powerfully, quite, really, remarkably, terribly, terrifically, utterly

A Lot

abundant, ample, bountiful, copious, countless, heaps, host, infinite, limitless, masses, multitudinous, myriad, numerous, overflowing, plentiful, swarms

A Little

few, infrequent, inconsiderable, negligent, minimal, sparse, scarce, meager, scanty, skimpy, scattered

Fast

abrupt, accelerated, agile, cursory, fleeting, hasty, hurried, immediate, impetuous, impulsive, instantaneous, momentary, nimble, prompt, quick, rapid, rash, ready, rushed, speedy, sudden, supersonic, swift, urgent

Slow

arrested, belated, delayed, deliberate, dormant, gradual, impeded, inert, lackadaisical, late, leisurely, lethargic, moderate, overdue, postponed, relaxed, reluctant, sluggish, tardy, tentative, unhurried

Good/Nice/Great

advantageous, appropriate, auspicious, beneficial, captivating, choice, competent, convenient, correct, decent, delectable, delicious, delightful, effective, enjoyable, excellent, exemplary, exquisite, fair, fascinating, favorable, functional, gratifying, healthy, helpful, honorable, interesting, just, legitimate, likable, magnificent, marvelous, proper, pleasant, practical, praiseworthy, precise, proficient, promising, pure, rewarding, satisfying, savory, select, sensational, skillful, sublime, superb, superior, supreme, terrific, unsurpassed, useful, valid, valuable, wonderful, worthwhile, worthy

Bad

atrocious, contaminated, corrupt, dangerous, decayed, deplorable, destructive, detestable, detrimental, disgusting, disorderly, disruptive, dreadful, erroneous, evil, feverish, foreboding, foul, harmful, hazardous, heinous, horrid, hurtful, ill, inaccurate, infamous, inferior, malignant, menacing, misbehaved, mischievous, naughty, nauseous, nefarious, noxious, odious, offensive, ominous, perilous, pitiful, putrid, queasy, rancid, reprehensible, repulsive, rotten, shameful, sick, sinister, spoiled, terrible, threatening, toxic, unfavorable, unhealthy, unlucky, unpleasant, unsafe, vicious, vile, worthless, wrong

Hot

balmy, blistering, boiling, burning, equatorial, feverish, fiery, flushed, glowing, humid, molten, muggy, parched, radiant, roasting, scorching, sizzling, steamy, sticky, stuffy, sultry, summery, sunny, sweaty, sweltering, thermal, toasty, torrid, tropical, warm

Cold

arctic, biting, bitter, blasting, bleak, blustery, breezy, brisk, chilly, cool, crisp, fresh, frigid, frosty, frozen, glacial, gusty, icy, inclement, numbing, overcast, raw, sleeting, slushy, snowy, subzero, turbulent, wintry

THESAURUS

Light/Sunny

aglow, alight, beaming, blaring, blazing, blinding, blinking, bouncing, bright, brilliant, clear, dazzling, flaming, flaring, flashing, flickering, fluorescent, glaring, gleaming, glimmering, glinting, glistening, glittering, glossy, glowing, illuminating, incandescent, iridescent, lucid, luminous, lustrous, radiant, scintillating, shimmering, shiny, sparkling, translucent, twinkling, vivid, winking

Dark/Cloudy

bleak, dim, drab, dull, eclipsed, foggy, gloaming, gloomy, hazy, lackluster, misty, murky, nebulous, obscure, overcast, shadowed, shady, shrouded, smoggy, somber, stormy, veiled

Loud

applause, banging, blaring, blasting, boisterous, booming, buzzing, cacophonous, cheering, chiming, clamorous, clashing, crashing, deafening, drilling, droning, ear-splitting, grating, pounding, rattling, resounding, roaring, rowdy, rumbling, screaming, shattering, sonorous, thumping, tumultuous, uproarious, vociferous

Quiet

faint, hushed, inaudible, indistinct, muffled, muted, peaceful, placid, restful, serene, silent, softened, stifled, still, subdued, tacit, whispered

Soft/Smooth

brushed, cushioned, delicate, doughy, downy, elastic, feathery, fleecy, flexible, flimsy, fluffy, furry, gentle, giving, glassy, glazed, glossy, paved, pliant, plush, polished, rubbery, satiny, shiny, silky, sleek, slick, slippery, soapy, soggy, spongy, springy, squishy, supple, tender, uniform, varnished, velvety, waxed, woolly

Hard/Rough

bony, bumpy, calcified, callous, coarse, concrete, congealed, craggy, crinkly, crisp, crude, crumpled, dense, encrusted, firm, flinty, gnarled, gritty, jagged, knotted, leathery, lumpy, marbleized, osseous, petrified, raw, rigid, rocky, ruffled, rugged, rumpled, scaly, scorched, scraggly, solid, steely, stiff, stony, sturdy, textured, tough, withered, wrinkled

Wet

clammy, damp, dewy, drenched, dripping, gooey, greasy, humid, moist, oozy, pulpy, runny, saturated, slimy, slippery, soaking, soggy, sopping, spongy, squishy, sticky, sweaty, syrupy, watery

Dry

arid, baked, brittle, chalky, dehydrated, desiccated, dusty, evaporated, faded, flaky, parched, powdered, scaly, scorched, seared, shriveled, withered

Colors

Black

coal, ebony, ink, jet black, licorice, obsidian, raven, sable

Blue

aqua, azure, cerulean, cobalt, cyan, electric blue, indigo, midnight, navy, peacock blue, royal blue, sapphire, sky blue, teal, turquoise, ultramarine

Brown

almond, bronze, brownstone, brunette, camel, caramel, chestnut, chocolate, cinnamon, coffee, copper, cordovan, fawn, khaki, mahogany, manila, maple, mink, mocha, molasses, rust, sandy, sepia, sienna, tan, tawny, toast, toffee, umber, walnut

Gray

ash, charcoal, chrome, flint, granite, lead, mousy, silver, slate, smoke, steel, taupe

Green

avocado, celadon, chartreuse, emerald, forest green, hazel, jade, kelly green, lime, mint, olive, pea green, sea green, hazel

Orange

amber, apricot, brassy, bronze, ginger, ochre, pumpkin, tangerine, terra cotta, topaz

THESAURUS

Pink
blush, coral, flamingo, fuchsia, mauve, peach, salmon

Purple
amethyst, fuchsia, grape, indigo, lavender, lilac, lily, magenta, orchid, plum, puce, violet

Red
Bordeaux, brick, burgundy, cardinal, cherry, claret, coral, crimson, garnet, magenta, maroon, mulberry, raspberry, rose, ruby, russet, rust, salmon, scarlet, strawberry, vermilion

White
alabaster, beige, bone, chalk, cream, ecru, eggshell, ivory, milky, mushroom, oatmeal, pearl, platinum, putty, silver, snow

Yellow
banana, beige, brass, canary, champagne, chartreuse, citron, cream, flax, gilded, golden, honey, lemon, mustard, saffron, sallow, sand, tawny

How People **Look**

Pretty/Handsome/Cute

adorable, alluring, appealing , attractive, beautiful, becoming, breathtaking, captivating, charismatic, charming, chic, classy, dashing, dazzling, dignified, elegant, enchanting, exquisite, fashionable, glamorous, gorgeous, groomed, heavenly, irresistible, lovely, magnificent, presentable, ravishing, splendid, striking, stunning, stylish

Big/Tall

ample, behemoth, blimpy, blubbery, brawny, broad, bulky, buxom, capacious, chubby, colossal, corpulent, elongated, enormous, fleshy, gargantuan, gigantic, goliath, heavyset, hefty, herculean, huge, husky, immense, imposing, long-legged, lumbering, mammoth, massive, mighty, obese, overweight, plump, pudgy, puffy, rotund, round, stocky, stout, swollen, thick, titanic, towering, tremendous, voluminous, wide

Small/Short

bony, compact, dainty, diminutive, frail, gangly, gawky, lanky, lean, meager, measly, miniature, narrow, petite, scant, scrawny, shriveled, shrunken, slender, slight, slim, small, stringy, thin, underweight, wiry

Old

adult, aged, ancient, decrepit, elderly, experienced, frail, gray, grizzled, mature, senior, shriveled, venerable, veteran, wise, withered, wrinkled

Young

adolescent, babyish, boyish, childlike, fledgling, girlish, immature, innocent, juvenile, minor, naive, teenager, underage, youthful

THESAURUS

How People **Act**

Nice

accommodating, acquiescent, affectionate, agreeable, altruistic, amiable, angelic, approachable, ardent, benevolent, charitable, charming, chummy, compassionate, compatible, comradely, conscientious, considerate, cooperative, cordial, courteous, decent, delightful, easygoing, enjoyable, favorable, forgiving, friendly, gallant, generous, genial, gentle, graceful, gracious, hearty, helpful, honest, hospitable, humble, intimate, kind, likable, loving, loyal, mild, neighborly, patient, personable, pleasant, polite, reliable, sensitive, sincere, sociable, sunny, sweet, sympathetic, tender, thoughtful, trusting, understanding, warm, welcoming

Mean

abrasive, angry, argumentative, arrogant, audacious, bitter, blunt, brazen, brutal, callous, cantankerous, catty, contemptuous, cynical, disrespectful, dour, egocentric, envious, formidable, frigid, greedy, harsh, hateful, impolite, inconsiderate, insensitive, insolent, intolerant, irritable, manipulative, menacing, obnoxious, offensive, oppressive, pompous, reprehensible, rude, ruthless, scornful, selfish, sneering, sour, spiteful, surly, thoughtless, uncivil, vengeful, venomous, vindictive

Outgoing/Funny

amusing, assertive, bubbly, comical, dramatic, dynamic, emphatic, extroverted, exuberant, facetious, fatuous, flamboyant, foolish, forward, frivolous, gregarious, hilarious, humorous, jocular, overbearing, overt, perky, playful, raucous, sarcastic, silly, talkative, uninhibited, verbose, vivacious, vocal, whimsical, witty

Shy/Serious

aloof, austere, bashful, calm, cautious, composed, conservative, consistent, constrained, covert, discreet, distant, inhibited, insipid, intense, introverted, isolated, nonchalant, passive, reclusive, remote, reserved, sedate, severe, sober, stern, stiff, strict, stuffy, taciturn, tedious, tranquil, withdrawn

Strong (Body or Mind)

adamant, adventurous, assured, authoritative, bold, bossy, brash, brave, brawny, confident, courageous, daring, decisive, determined, domineering, egotistic, fearless, focused, headstrong, imperious, independent, indestructible, insistent, intimidating, intrepid, invincible, mighty, muscular, obdurate, obstinate, opinionated, persuasive, powerful, proud, resilient, resolute, self-confident, steadfast, stubborn, valiant

Weak (Body or Mind)

anemic, apprehensive, brittle, concessive, cowardly, craven, debilitated, delicate, dependent, doubtful, downtrodden, exposed, faint, faltering, feeble, fragile, helpless, humbled, incredulous, insecure, meager, obsequious, reluctant, sheepish, subdued, submissive, subservient, susceptible, vulnerable, weary

How People **Feel**

Happy

amused, beaming, blissful, bright, buoyant, carefree, cheerful, comfortable, content, delighted, ecstatic, elated, enchanted, enjoyable, entranced, euphoric, exuberant, festive, fulfilled, genial, gentle, glowing, gratified, jolly, jovial, joyful, jubilant, lively, optimistic, overjoyed, perky, pleased, radiant, satisfied, sparkling, spirited, sunny

Sad

abysmal, aching, afflicted, agonized, anguished, bereaved, blue, brooding, crushed, dejected, depressed, desolate, despondent, disconcerted, discouraged, dismal, distressed, disturbed, down, dreary, droopy, glum, grieved, grim, homesick, hurt, inconsolable, joyless, lonely, low, melancholy, miserable, morose, nostalgic, oppressed, perturbed, pessimistic, pitiful, remorseful, ruffled, solemn, sorrowful, suffering, sullen, tormented, troubled, uncomfortable, uneasy, unfortunate, unfulfilled, upset, wistful

Angry

aggravated, aggressive, annoyed, belligerent, bitter, competitive, contentious, cranky, cross, disagreeable, enraged, exasperated, ferocious, fierce, fuming, furious, gruff, impassioned, incensed, indignant, irascible, irate, irked, irritated, livid, ornery, raving, resentful, scowling, seething, sour, surly, temperamental, tempestuous, testy, troubled, upset, visceral, wrathful

Bored

apathetic, blasé, complacent, dazed, detached, disinterested, dormant, dreamy, drooping, idle, inattentive, indifferent, inert, listless, oblivious, passive, sedentary, stagnant, unconcerned, unconscious, unmotivated, vacuous

Excited

animated, avid, breathless, brisk, curious, eager, effervescent, enthralled, enthusiastic, exhilarated, explosive, fascinated, feisty, frenzied, intent, intrigued, jolted, motivated, moved, passionate, restless, shaken, spellbound, spontaneous

Scared

afraid, aghast, alarmed, anxious, apprehensive, fearful, frightened, horrified, incapacitated, jittery, mortified, panicked, paranoid, petrified, squeamish, terrified, terrorized, timorous, trembling, unnerved

Surprised

astonished, amazed, astounded, dumbfounded, stupefied, bewildered, startled, staggered, perplexed, shocked, jarred, shaken

Friends and Relatives

aunt, brother, brother-in-law, cousin, daughter, daughter-in-law, father, dad, daddy, father-in-law, granddaughter, grandfather, grandpa, grandmother, grandma, grandparent, grandson, granny, great-grandfather, great-grandmother, great-grandparent, half brother, half sister, husband, in-law, mother, mom, mommy, mama, mother-in-law, nana, nephew, niece, sibling, parent, sister, sister-in-law, son, son-in-law, spouse, stepbrother, stepsister, stepfather, stepdad, stepmother, stepmom, stepparent, stepson, stepdaughter, uncle, wife, partner, guardian, neighbor, best friend, roommate, classmate, baby-sitter, coworker, boyfriend, girlfriend, fiancée, buddy, teammate, mentor

Words to Use When You Write about Actions

Said

announced, articulated, barked, bellowed, blurted out, cackled, called, commented, complained, cried, declared, enunciated, exclaimed, explained, exploded, gasped, hissed, interrupted, laughed, mentioned, moaned, mumbled, murmured, muttered, pronounced, remarked, repeated, roared, screamed, screeched, shouted, shrieked, sighed, snapped, snarled, snickered, spoke, squawked, stated, uttered, whimpered, whined, whispered, yelled

Asked

challenged, demanded, doubted, inquired, inspected, interrogated, polled, probed, pried, queried, questioned, quizzed, requested, reviewed, scanned, scrutinized, searched, sought, studied, surveyed, wondered

Replied

addressed, announced, answered, declared, interjected, refuted, rejoined, remarked, responded, retorted

Come/Came

accompany, advance, appear, approach, arrive, barge, commute, emerge, enter, find, immigrate, intrude, land, migrate, obtrude, pioneer, reach, return, settle, surface, trespass, visit

Go/Went

bolt, bound, bustle, catapult, charge, creep, cruise, dart, dash, dawdle, depart, desert, drift, embark, emigrate, escape, exit, float, flutter, fly, gallop, glide, hike, hobble, hop, hurry, hustle, jet, jog, journey, jump, lead, leap, lumber, march, plow, proceed, prowl, pursue, race, ramble, retreat, run, rush, sail, saunter, scamper, scramble, scurry, shuffle, skip, slide, sneak, soar, speed, sprint, stagger, stomp, stray, stride, stroll, strut, swagger, swarm, swim, tiptoe, travel, trudge, walk, wander, zip

Get

accept, acquire, attain, capture, clutch, collect, earn, gain, grab, grasp, inherit, obtain, possess, receive, secure, seize, snatch, steal, take, win

Give

award, bestow, confer, deliver, donate, entertain, grant, lend, offer, present, provide, render, reward, sacrifice, share, supply, transfer, treat

Eat/Drink

bite, binge, chew, consume, crunch, devour, engulf, feed, gnaw, gobble, gorge, graze, grind, gulp, ingest, lap, pick, munch, nibble, savor, sip, slurp, snack, swallow, swig, taste

Like/Love

accept, acclaim, acknowledge, acquiesce, admire, adore, applaud, appreciate, approve, cherish, complement, comply, cooperate, credit, desire, empathize, endorse, enjoy, esteem, fancy, glorify, harmonize, honor, idolize, praise, prefer, prize, recognize, reconcile, regard, relish, respect, revere, sympathize, treasure, understand, validate, value, welcome, worship

Dislike/Hate

abhor, antagonize, battle, begrudge, bicker, brawl, challenge, clash, compete, conflict, confront, contest, contradict, counter, debate, defy, despise, detest, dispute, embitter, feud, loathe, oppose, protest, quarrel, reject, resist, rival, scorn, spite, squabble

Make

combine, compile, compose, connect, construct, create, design, erect, form, join, manufacture, plan, put together, unite

Break

abolish, annihilate, damage, demolish, destruct, eradicate, exterminate, extinguish, harm, impair, injure, purge, ruin, sabotage, sink, terminate, vaporize

See/Look

examine, gape, gawk, gaze, glare, glimpse, inspect, leer, monitor, observe, ogle, peek, peep, scan, scout, scowl, scrutinize, squint, stare, study, supervise, survey, view

Think

brainstorm, concentrate, conceptualize, conjecture, consider, contemplate, deduce, dream, imagine, learn, meditate, perceive, philosophize, ponder, rationalize, reason, reflect, speculate, study, theorize, wonder

Write

characterize, compose, describe, dramatize, express, narrate, pen, portray, recount, represent, tell

THESAURUS

Words to Use When You Write about Places

Continents & Countries

Africa

Algeria
Angola
Benin
Botswana
Burkina
Burundi
Cameroon
Cape Verde
Central African
  Republic
Chad
Comoros
Congo
Djibouti
Egypt
Equatorial Guinea
Eritrea
Ethiopia
Gabon
Gambia
Ghana
Guinea
Guinea-Bissau
Ivory Coast
Kenya
Lesotho

Liberia
Libya
Madagascar
Malawi
Mali
Mauritania
Mauritius
Morocco
Mozambique
Namibia
Niger
Nigeria
Rwanda
Sao Tome and
  Principe
Senegal
Seychelles
Sierra Leone
Somalia
South Africa
Sudan
Swaziland
Tanzania
Togo
Tunisia
Uganda
Zambia
Zimbabwe

Asia

Afghanistan
Armenia
Azerbaijan
Bahrain
Bangladesh
Bhutan
Brunei
Burma (Myanmar)
Cambodia
China
Cyprus
India
Indonesia
Iran
Iraq
Israel
Japan
Jordan
Kazakhstan
Kuwait
Kyrgyzstan
Laos
Lebanon
Malaysia
Maldives
Mongolia

	Australia/Oceania	Europe
Nepal	Australia	Albania
North Korea	Fiji	Andorra
Oman	Kiribati	Austria
Pakistan	Marshall Islands	Belarus
Philippines	Micronesia	Belgium
Qatar	Nauru	Bosnia-
Russian Federation	New Zealand	Herzegovina
Saudi Arabia	Palau	Bulgaria
Singapore	Papua New Guinea	Croatia
South Korea	Samoa	Czech Republic
Sri Lanka	Solomon Islands	Denmark
Syria	Tonga	Estonia
Taiwan	Tuvalu	Finland
Tajikistan	Vanuatu	France
Thailand		Georgia
Turkey		Germany
Turkmenistan		Greece
United Arab		Hungary
Emirates		Iceland
Uzbekistan		Ireland
Vietnam		Italy
Yemen		Latvia
		Liechtenstein
		Lithuania
		Luxembourg
		Macedonia
		Malta
		Moldova

Monaco

The Netherlands

Norway

Poland

Portugal

Romania

San Marino

Serbia/Montenegro
(Yugoslavia)

Slovakia

Slovenia

Spain

Sweden

Switzerland

Ukraine

United Kingdom

Vatican City

North America

Antigua and
Barbuda

Bahamas

Barbados

Belize

Canada

Costa Rica

Cuba

Dominica

Dominican
Republic

El Salvador

Grenada

Guatemala

Haiti

Honduras

Jamaica

Mexico

Nicaragua

Panama

St. Kitts and Nevis

St. Lucia

St. Vincent and the
Grenadines

Trinidad & Tobago

The United States
of America
(U.S.A)

South America

Argentina

Bolivia

Brazil

Chile

Colombia

Ecuador

Guyana

Paraguay

Peru

Suriname

Uruguay

Venezuela

The United States, Territories, & Abbreviations

Alabama (AL)

Alaska (AK)

American Samoa (AS)

Arizona (AZ)

Arkansas (AR)

California (CA)

Colorado (CO)

Connecticut (CT)

Delaware (DE)

District of Columbia (DC)

Federated States Of Micronesia (FM)

Florida (FL)

Georgia (GA)

Guam (GU)

Hawaii (HI)

Idaho (ID)

Illinois (IL)

Indiana (IN)

Iowa (IA)

Kansas (KS)

Kentucky (KY)

Louisiana (LA)

Maine (ME)

Marshall Islands (MH)

Maryland (MD)

Massachusetts (MA)

Michigan (MI)

Minnesota (MN)

Mississippi (MS)

Missouri (MO)

Montana (MT)

Nebraska (NE)

Nevada (NV)

New Hampshire (NH)

New Jersey (NJ)

New Mexico (NM)

New York (NY)

North Carolina (NC)

North Dakota (ND)

Northern Mariana Islands (MP)

Ohio (OH)

Oklahoma (OK)

Oregon (OR)

Palau (PW)

Pennsylvania (PA)

Puerto Rico (PR)

Rhode Island (RI)

South Carolina (SC)

South Dakota (SD)

Tennessee (TN)

Texas (TX)

Utah (UT)

Vermont (VT)

Virgin Islands (VI)

Virginia (VA)

Washington (WA)

West Virginia (WV)

Wisconsin (WI)

Wyoming (WY)

Canadian Provinces, Territories, & Abbreviations

Alberta (AB)

British Columbia (BC)

Manitoba (MB)

New Brunswick (NB)

Newfoundland (NF)

Northwest Territories (NT)

Nova Scotia (NS)

Nunavut (NU)

Ontario (ON)

Prince Edward Island (PE)

Quebec (QC)

Saskatchewan (SK)

Yukon (YT)

THESAURUS

Words to Use When You Write About

Religions

Amish

Anglican

Baptist

Buddhism, Buddhist

Catholicism, Catholic

Christian Science, Christian Scientist

Christianity, Christian

Confucianism

Congregational

Eastern Orthodox

Episcopal

Greek Orthodox

Hasidism, Hasidic

Hinduism, Hindu

Islam, Muslim

Jainism

Jehovah's Witnesses

Judaism, Jewish

Lutheran

Mennonite

Methodist

Mormon

Presbyterian

Puritan

Quaker

Russian Orthodox

Shaker

Shamanism, Shaman

Shintoism, Shinto

Sikhism, Sikh

Taoism, Tao

Unitarian

Unitarian-Universalist

Universalist

Zen, Zen Buddhist

National and Religious Holidays

April Fools' Day

Arab League Day

Arbor Day

Bastille Day
(France)

Canada Day

Chinese New Year

Christmas

Cinco de Mayo
(Mexico)

Columbus Day

Diwali (Hindu)

Easter

Election Day

Father's Day

Groundhog day

Halloween

Hanukkah

Human Rights Day

Independence Day
(Israel, Mexico,
U.S.)

Kwanzaa

Labor Day

Mardi Gras

Martin Luther King
Day

Memorial Day

Moharram
(Islamic)

Mother's Day

National Day
(China, Spain)

New Year's Day

Omisoka (Japan)

Passover

Presidents' Day

Queen's Birthday
(Great Britain)

Ramadan (Islamic)

Republic Day
(India)

Rosh Hashanah

Saint Patrick's Day

Tet (Vietnam)

Thanksgiving Day

Valentine's Day

Veteran's Day

Yom Kippur

THESAURUS

Words to Use When You Write about Computers & Technology

application

backup

bookmark

browser

bug

bulletin board

byte

cache

CD

CD burner

CD-ROM

chat

chip

click

command

configuration

CPU (central processing unit)

crash

cursor

cut

cyberspace

data

default

desktop

dial-up

digital

digital camera

directory

disk

domain

double-click

download

drive

e-mail

emoticon

error message

exit

extension

FAQ (frequently asked questions)

file

floppy disk

folder

font

graphics

hard copy

hardware

home page

HTML (hypertext markup language)

HTTP (hypertext transfer protocol)

hypertext

icon

input

Intel

interactive

interface

Internet

ISP (internet service provider)

Java

keyboard

laptop

link

listserv

load

load

Mac (Macintosh)

mailbox

memory

menu

modem

module

monitor

motherboard

mouse

multimedia

network

newsgroup

online

118

operating system

paste

patch

PC (personal computer)

PDA (personal digital assistant)

Pentium

peripheral

pixel

plug-and-play

post

printer

program

queue

quit

RAM (random access memory)

refresh

resolution

save

scanner

screen saver

scrolling

search engine

server

site

software

spam

surf

toolbar

undo

upgrade

upload

URL (universal resource locator)

virus

Web cam

window

word processor

www (World Wide Web)

zip drive

zip/unzip

Words to Use When You Write about Sports & Activities

aerobics

aikido

archery

badminton

baseball

basketball

bobsled

body building

bowling

boxing

canoeing

cricket

curling

cycling

diving

dodge ball

fencing

figure skating

fishing

footbag (hacky sack)

football

golf

gymnastics

handball

hang gliding

hiking

hockey

horseback riding

jai alai

jogging

jujitsu

karate

kayaking

kick boxing

kickball

kung fu

lacrosse

luge

miniature golf

parasailing

polo

racquetball

rafting

rock climbing

rollerblading
  (inline skating)

rowing (crew)

rugby

running bases

running

step aerobics

scuba diving

skateboarding

skiing

sky-diving

snowboarding

soccer

softball

speed skating

squash

stickball

surfing

swimming

synchronized
  swimming

ta'i chi

table tennis
  (ping pong)

tae kwon do

T-ball

tennis

track and field

volleyball

water polo

water skiing

weightlifting

wiffle ball

wrestling

yoga

_____

_____

accountant

actor, actress

advertiser

air traffic controller

ambassador

archaeologist

architect

artist

astronaut

athletic trainer

attorney (lawyer)

baker

bank teller

banker

biologist

biologist

blacksmith

bookkeeper

broadcaster

building contractor

bus driver

butcher

carpenter

cashier

chauffeur

chef

chemist

child care worker

chiropractor

clergy

coach

composer

computer programmer

computer technician

conductor

construction worker

cosmetologist

counselor

courier

curator

custodian

dancer

deejay

dental hygienist

dentist

designer

dietitian

director

dispatcher

doctor

editor

electrician

emergency medical technician

engineer

executive

farmer

fashion designer

financial planner

firefighter

fisher

fitness instructor

flight attendant

forester

gardener

groundskeeper

hair dresser

historian

illustrator

insurance agent

interpreter

investigator

jeweler

journalist

judge

law enforcement officer

librarian

mail carrier

maintenance worker

mason

massage therapist

mathematician

mechanic

medical assistant

meteorologist

miner

models

musician

newscaster

nurse

office manager

optician

optometrist

orthodontist

painter

pediatrician

pharmacist

photographer

physical therapist

physician

physicist

pilot

plumber

politician

postal clerk

professional athlete

psychologist

psychiatrist

publicist

railroad conductor

real estate agent

receptionist

repairperson

reporter

roofer

salesperson

sanitation worker

scientist

security guard

singer

social worker

stenographer

stockbroker

superintendent

surgeon

tailor

taxi driver

teacher

telephone operator

translator

travel agent

truck driver

tutor

urban planner

veterinarian

webmaster

writer

THESAURUS

Index

Index

INDEX